CONTENTS

A MANIFESTO FOR A KINDER POLITICS

Why Marxism needs religion and why relationships matter

Jonathan Smith

Jonathan Smith

To Danny, Jacob and Raven. With love and hope for peace and friendship.

FORWARD

The origin of what I have come to call a 'Manifesto for a Kinder Politics' has its roots in the frustration with knowing that we desperately need to do things differently. The ways we have done things in the past, and at present, no longer work. A new story is needed if we are to change the world into a reality that we, with the rest of the world, can happily inhabit. By a story I don't mean to imply the truth or not of what is said but rather an explanation of how we account for who we are and what we stand for. (1) Stories are not always clearly articulated and are often interpreted differently. This becomes clear if we consider some of the big stories that have served.

Two of the longest serving, in our culture, are the Christmas and Easter Stories. The broad outline of these stories is widely known with their central characters, under God, being Jesus, Mary, and the disciples. I don't say this with any hint of disparagement but rather to identify the bones upon which there is still consensus for believers and non-believers alike. Yet, an effective story needs to touch us all if we are to proceed harmoniously together.

However, if we take the Christian story and delve a little deeper the story begins to fragment and fails to bring us or hold us together. Of course, Christianity in all its various shades is not the only big story on the block the next five major world religions, in terms of membership claimed, are Islam, Hinduism, Buddhism, Sikhism and Judaism. Like Christianity there are numerous sub stories some complementing, many competing to be the story. (2)

There are of course other less widely known stories, but which are still central to millions of people lives. Such stories can be both religious and non-religious and reflect the rich diversity of our human inheritance. However, we now live in a global world where a fall in The Dow, a shut down in Shanghai or an outbreak of Ebola, or rising sea levels and erratic weather all connect in different ways which affect people, animals and our environment. There are also layered political conflicts around perceived and actual scarce resources from oil, water, food, clean air, health, housing and education. In a global world the stories need connecting. For, as we have seen, if the big stories no longer resonate then lesser stories, one-sided, non-inclusive stories claim authority usually with disastrous consequences. From the holocaust to the gulags, from modern slavery to widespread unemployment, from the degradation of the environment to mass extinctions and famine in a world of plenty. We clearly need a new story to help navigate us out of the mess.

The story you hold is to others possibly quaint or more perniciously regarded as an ideology that claims sovereignty of both its adherents and frequently, everyone else. Yet, such political and economic stories or ideologies rise and fall. Recently, in the last century, we have witnessed fascism, Keynesianism, monetarism and Marxism. They are all stories, political and economic, that have in some form or other held both power and widespread attention. Yet, have generally been found wanting. Today, it's neoliberalism which is tearing our communities apart.

All the stories identified above, except for Marxism, are shades of what we know as capitalism. Yet, Marxism, whilst identifying capitalism as the historical culprit that needs transforming has still failed to unite the people of the world. One reason may be because its own story is fragmented, there is not one voice but many which are also locked in competition to become the story just like the competition between the larger religious stories. In all cases the reality I think we would like to inhabit, one of love, justice and equality, is forsaken and instead we are served labels. Others are traitors, betrayers, careerists, exploiters, racists, sexists and even heretics. That is not to say, of course that all those traits don't exist, they do but not exclusively, we all have our shadows, and one person's traitor can be another person's hero or heroine.

Yet, neither, would I conclude from all this that such stories are relative, for me that is self-contradictory. It states what it cannot- a truth. However, whilst we may not be able to claim the truth, it is something I think we can work towards. So, the story we so badly need is something we need to work towards. For, a story, as George Monbiot argues in 'Out of The Wreckage' can only be replaced by another story. (3) This manifesto is another modest contribution to the further creation of that story. Its focus is not just on what we need to do but as importantly how we do it. I hope you find it stimulating.

Jon Smith Rotherham January 2019

1 George Monbiot 2018 p2

2. hhtps://www.infoplease.com>religion (16.00 4/1/19)

3. George Monbiot 2018 p3

INTRODUCTION

A way towards universal justice

It is my intention to show how religion is crucial for progressive social change. This contrasts with many on the left who see religion as one of the problems rather than the solution. Indeed, Marxists see religion as an obstacle to be overcome rather than a way of achieving their goals of an equal and just society. Yet, religion too, shares these goals of justice and equality.

Further, whilst I accept that there are widespread and negative interpretations of religion, just as there are negative and conflicting interpretations of Marxism I, nevertheless, argue that we are at root religious beings. I will examine the view of religion as espoused by Marx, I will also examine some of the evidence to support and challenge Marx's view of religion before asking the reader to look at religion in a different, perhaps even a revolutionary way.

This requires being introduced to a new logic. Generally, if not always consciously, we are familiar with formal positivist logic. This refers to the relations of cause and effect which underpin the sciences that deal with the physical world or inorganic world and what we understand by objectivity and science. Many, though fewer, are also familiar with our understanding of the logic of the organic world which deals with plants and animals. This was the logic embraced in the dialectics of Hegel and Marx; the logic which underpins the development or the evolution of living organisms. However, what is different is the logic of the personal. This, at source, is what, characterises the religious world: How we treat each other. The failure to acknowledge and consciously recognise the logic of the personal has hampered attempts to bring about genuine social change. For me, it is like a machine firing on two cylinders instead of three, making positive change that much more difficult. An integrated approach, acknowledging the logic of the personal, is more likely to enable change as all avenues for development are harnessed and recognised.

The insights of the Personal are those of a Scottish Philosopher, popular between the two world wars, called John Macmurray (1891-1976). He wrote extensively and clearly. His work focuses attention on the personal but not to be confused with the person centred psychology of Carl Rogers and others. John Macmurray focuses on humans in relationship but as the recognised core of religion; a view contemporaneously expressed by Christian theologians such as Richard Rohr, Cynthia Bourgeault and Karen Armstrong who, among others, seek to reconstruct our understanding of religion by focusing on the personal.

Religion itself is evolving, like the universe and all within it. However, the understanding of religion will always reflect the level of consciousness present at any era in history. For millennia, the consciousness of humanity placed 'God' out there in the beyond, but Richard Rohr and many other religious scholars argue that the reality we call God can be experienced both outside and inside. This has been expressed by all who have said that 'God is love' and if part of the mystery we understand by God is love, then loving, which is not an object, can only be fully expressed in relationship.

Marx once claimed he was not a Marxist due to the many corrupt and misleading readings of his work. If Jesus walked the earth today, I am convinced he would be appalled at many of those who call themselves Christian. Consequently, it is important to look beyond labels and try to fathom the core meanings which can inspire us to action and live in harmony with others and the world we inhabit

We live in exciting times. Seismic shifts are reconstructing the political landscape presenting both opportunities and dangers. In Britain we are witnessing the shakeup of the Labour Party. Internationally, new parties are erupting on the scene. For me Jeremy Corbyn's proposal for a kinder politics – and others who agree with him - is not only more respectful but necessary to enable a new age to be born, which would be more open, democratic, equal and just.

I hope that many people will read this Manifesto, that the relationship between politics and religion can be reframed productively and creatively. I also hope that it honours its claim to be a Manifesto; to be clear and easily understood. Nevertheless, some of the ideas may not be easily grasped at a first reading. Yet, as a Manifesto, it is for everybody who wishes to see a more equal and just world. Though it particularly addresses those who currently or in the past have or had sympathies with Marx, it also addresses those people who 'know' there is something larger than us and our own ego consciousness, however, we wish to express this. Finally, it is also addressed to those within established religious organisations, who have faith and the desire to connect. Who wish to share a faith that includes living in a more just world where bread is shared more equitably than now.

WE ARE RELIGIOUS BEINGS

Professor Roger Trigg from Oxford University argues that "we have gathered a body of evidence that suggests that religion is a common fact of human nature across different societies". (Ross 2011) Evidence for religious belief goes back at least 50,000 to 100,000 years and nearly, every known human culture has creation myths. (Stavrakcopoulou F) It is currently estimated 84% of the world's population today are members of religious groups or claim that religion is important in their lives. (Stavrakcopoulou F) However, Richard Hawkins and other atheists, including Marx, believe that religion is all a delusion, yet they are unable to realistically account for the persistence of beliefs that they denounce as poisonously irrational. (Gray 2016)

However, for this project, I invite you to accept that religion, in its various forms, has persisted and continues to persist alongside human advances in science and technology as well as in art and other forms of creativity.

Yet, science, as John Macmurray emphasised, "cannot save the world since it must serve and cannot lead" (1936 p10). Science can help us get what we want, for example a nuclear bomb but it cannot help us decide if that is the best course of action. So, science provides the means, and generally very effective ones, but not ends. Indeed, some of the best scientists are ironically creating ever more sophisticated means for our destruction. Possibly not the end we would collectively or rationally desire?

Further, in part, to keep professed 'atheists' on board; "just as the field of science is the whole body of common fact, which it is the scientists endeavour to understand, so religion must also have as its ground and starting point the facts of human experience" (1936 p13). Clearly, the success of the telephone was only possible through a true understanding of science. If the science was wrong the phone wouldn't work. However, the falsification of religion that matters most is not the ultimate truth or falsity of beliefs but the reference of these beliefs to experience. (1936 p60) In this sense religion, at its best, must abandon dogmatism and become empirical. In the way Liberation theologists championed the poor both in word and action. This points to a radically different perspective on Religion, grounded in experience. [Indeed, for Macmurray if "religion is found still on the side of reaction, as it was in Russia (in 1917), it must suffer almost total eclipse" (1936 p9).]

Clearly, religion does arise from human experience. So, what are the facts which frame the religious mind? Selection necessarily involves valuation.

What science values is utilitarian; it focuses on what is measured and counted, and with further reflection moves from individuality to generality. In contrast, art expresses intrinsic value, its attitude moves in the opposite direction toward individuality and uniqueness; we know, for example, that delight and beauty are ephemeral, so the artistic attitude can seek to immortalise those moments. Yet, *as human beings* we are both the source and object of valuation, we have both utility and intrinsic value. The attitude of mind that characterises both is that of religion.

For each of us the rest of us are data; that is your use to me. A scientific attitude. How we value the world, what value we have and how do we value each other reflects an artistic attitude. Their combination, which arises as soon as we do something-for example employ a worker-reflects the attitude of religion-for example, how we treat them the workers. Indeed, religious valuation is forced upon us by the necessity of being in relationships "Judge not, that ye be not judged". (1936 p25-29). Consequently, Macmurray argues that "The field of religion is the whole field of common experience organised in relation to the central fact of personal relationship…Religion is about fellowship and community, which are facts of direct, universal human experience." (1936 p30)

A person who has no religion has merely forgotten that humanity exists only in the relation of human beings to one another. Religion is the reflective aspect of a universal human experience. When community breaks down then a change of heart or mind is the condition of reconciliation. What is required is mutual forgiveness. Paradoxically, once the estrangement is overcome and sincere then it results in a strengthening of community. Unsurprisingly, the very words we use, such as forgiveness and reconciliation, are those we are familiar with in religion which, for Macmurray, is the primary expression of reason in human life.

Until relatively recently science, undeveloped and immature, sought the elixir of life or the philosophers stone, similar childish dreams in religion simply reflect religions' immaturity. The early function of religion was to extend family affection to wider groups, the tribe, the kingdom, the nation. Thus, the intentionality born from this reflection sought to continue relationships, the community, into the future, despite the deaths of its members. In our time the consciousness of community is, at its widest effective limit, national. Yet, the professed intention for the world's religions is universal brotherhood. (1936 p32-54) Sadly, the European Union has remained essentially an economic union and whilst some can identify with a European consciousness, it is not, as yet, sufficiently widespread to trump nationalism. Corporate brands also transcend national boundaries but are again essentially economic with no real concern for community except as a marketing or advertising tool.

Consequently, religion has the intention and potential to create a universal community. However, any reflection can be performed rightly or wrongly, in this sense religion can be either for good or for bad. Consequently, there is a need to distinguish between religious activities which are right and wrong, true or false, rational or sentimental and vicious. (1936 p56) For Macmurray religious doctrines are not rules for achieving things, such as an afterlife. Religion is about raising the level of reflective consciousness, to know what we are doing and to do it better. As said above it is not the ultimate truth or falsity of beliefs that matters most but rather the falsification of the reference of these beliefs to practice. Indeed, many ancient myths...were true in a sense that the people who believed them recognised them as referring quite properly to their own direct experience. Further, without an intentional reference to common experience, religious reflection is a meaningless play of imagination. Indeed, for a religion which simply refers to another world does not destroy reference to this world, but it becomes unconscious and dissociated whilst referring to the secular life of the community as it was at the time the dissociation set in. For the West this dissociation became chronic with the advent of mainstream science when scientific conclusions collided with the dogmatic pronouncements or edicts of the Church. In this way, a dissociated religion can work as a powerful conservative agency resistant to change. (1936 p59-68)

Fortunately, in its full unfolding, religious reflection reveals the possibility of a universal community of humankind, it only becomes mere sentiment and idea if there is no longer any effective intention of carrying into operation the actuality of economic inter-dependence by creating a universal community now. (1936 p74). Yet, we are one 'community' economically at least. Indeed, co-dependency is dramatically revealed during both strikes and restrictions on free trade.

In this section I have tried to show how central religion is in our lives as human beings in relationship living in communities. Religion is our operating system science and art are our tools to achieve and focus our intentions. Art, science, and religion are not in opposition but are a necessary aspect of a whole, that they seem fractured or disassociated is simply a reflection of what needs to be done. Next, we look at how Marxism rejected a distorted and deformed religion far removed from the compassion and freedom it promised.

RELIGION AS THE 'OPIUM OF THE PEOPLE'.

Marxism is a materialist philosophy. Marx turned Hegel's idealist philosophy on its head and promoted dialectical materialism as the method necessary to understand history and map a way forward for the working class and humanity in general. Indeed, socialism or barbarism are the striking alternatives for a history driven by the relentless unfolding of class conflict.

Marxism regards history as the necessary product of the contradiction between antagonistic social classes. Thus, within Capitalist society the ruling class exploit the working class. This is primarily an economic relationship where the capitalists' profit is extracted from the surplus value produced by the workers. Exploitation can be severe in times of crisis leaving people without the necessities to live a civilised life or more benign when the economy is buoyant, and wealth is shared more equitably; at least in the industrialised world. Yet, at times of crisis 'exploitation' takes on a moral judgment as people are clearly suffering, on the other hand, in boom times, whilst workers are still exploited economically, as consumers they are satiated, as standards of living rise and the system appears to work. [1]

For Marx the solution to the recurring economic crises is a workers' revolution where the dictatorship of the proletariat replaces the dictatorship of the bourgeoisie. This simply means the commanding heights of the economy such as the banks and major industries are controlled by the democratic majority rather than an elite, super rich, minority. The workers, most of the population, will control society and decide how its fruits will be distributed rather than the ruling class. However, within bourgeois democracy, something is stopping most of the population from uniting and replacing the ruling class. Marx calls this 'false consciousness', this means that the working class is not aware of its exploitation due to the dominance of 'ruling class' ideology. Marx explains this through his understanding of the role of the state.

For Marx the ideas of the ruling class become the dominant ideas by controlling the economic base of society; that is, they control the means of production, the factories, the commanding heights of the economy including the banks, utilities, and infrastructure. Controlling the economic base leads to control of the state superstructure, that is the government, civil service, armed forces, education system, justice system and media. These institutions reproduce and defend dominant class relations by promoting ruling class ideas; by getting us to believe they are right or that there is no alternative. That is the "ideas of the ruling class are in every age the ruling ideas". In the past this was, for Marxists, a fundamental role of the Church. [2]

Marx claims that religion focused the oppressed not in this life but the next; if you were good and followed the rules then your reward was in heaven. It further consoled people by helping to dull the pain of oppression, like opium - a drug which kills pain. Hence, Marx's pithy characterisation of religion as "the opium of the people". Lenin similarly regarded religion as the 'spiritual gin' necessary to mollify the grim reality of workers lives. Lastly, religion often justified the existing social order as 'God's will, so further helping to prevent social change. There is significant historical interpretation even evidence to support this Marxist view of religion from the Pharaohs of ancient Egypt to the present day. For example, the Church played a reactionary role in Russia in 1917 and in the Spanish civil war where it sided with Fascism and the military coup led by General Franco. In the past excommunication was also used as a tool to discipline dissent, and the current wealth and riches of the Catholic Church continue to stand in stark contrast to the life of the world's poor; its finely tuned hierarchies also promote inequality as inevitable and natural. [3]

However, whilst it is undeniable that religion at different moments in history has played this ideological and repressive role it is not the core of a Marxist criticism of religion. Indeed, as Engels and others have noted, religion can play a progressive role. For example, Christianity inspired Martin Luther King and Islam inspired Malcom X to mobilise for Civil Rights in America. (Molyneux 2008)) Further, the ideological function of religion has been largely superseded by the mass media and, Marxists argue, the education system. The pulpit is no longer the main conduit for informing the people in the industrialised world but for Marx religions continue to obfuscate the real relationships in society. Why is explained in the next section.

Notes

[1] Marxism has proved an enduring political philosophy despite the triumphalism of neo-liberalism. The end of history was never believable, its arrogance shallow and misleading. People continue to fight oppression and will find the human will to reject subjugation. Witness the ongoing Palestinian struggle for nationhood, for workers in South Africa demanding living wages and modern utilities. Indeed, for people across the world challenging the ruling classes intention to force workers to pay for the crisis. However, Marx dedicated his life, as a champion of the oppressed. His aim was to articulate an understanding of capitalism and chart a way forward.

Essentially, it was and remains Marxist economics. Initially developed in the mid nineteenth century, his work accurately captures how capitalism came about, how it develops and endures as well as delineating its future trajectories and possibilities. The choice for humanity was stark. Fidel Castro frequently finished his speeches with the cry 'Socialism or death' a modified form of the 'socialism or barbarism' of the earlier Marxists. It is beyond me to précis Marxist economics; sufficient to say that Marx, through the labour theory of values explains how workers, the proletariat, are exploited and why this is necessary for capitalism to endure and reproduce its profits. Further, whilst crises prior to capitalism were based on shortages today crises are of over production- there are seemingly too many workers, too many goods to be sold at a profit. Marx demonstrated how the competition for markets and natural resources has been the source of conflict between imperialist powers and continues to be the fundamental driver towards war. (1) His work is evidenced. His method is dialectical. In this sense Marx would regard himself as scientific, that his analysis of capitalism is objective.

It was Marx's understanding of economics, of capitalism, as a mode of production, as the economic force in society that he identified the working class, the proletariat, as not only the essential source of profits but also the core instrument for the transformation of society to socialism. Workers' desire to earn a living wage challenged the bourgeoisie, the owners of the factories, ability to maximise their profits. Maximisation of profit was essential, from their point of view, if they were to remain competitive. The exploitation of the proletariat is what underpins class conflict as workers attempt to claim a greater share of the surplus value they produce but is hijacked by the ruling class because they own the means of production. Production is collective, but the rich rewards are based on property ownership. Paradoxically, and contrary to common sense, workers are more exploited today, economically, than they were in the past because the labour time necessary to produce their 'wages' is less than it was in the past. The standard of living measured in terms of consumables has for long periods gone up but it takes a fraction of the labour time to produce those goods due to increases in productivity; for example - not too exciting I am afraid- a chair crafted in 1850 will have taken longer to produce than the mass produced chairs of today but now we all, for the most part, have chairs to sit on. Similarly, a loaf of bread, pork chops a bottle of wine or... pints of beer. Well now we are talking! Why do these exploitative relations continue? Marx also offers explanations for this based on historical materialism. A view of history based on material relations in society and not on spurious explanations like divine intervention or the will of great men and sometimes women. I say this not to diminish the role of women but simply as a recognition that they have largely been excluded or marginalised from what counts as 'history' (it's all in the name!). Clearly, they were and are part of history that this is not always apparent simply highlights the interpretative character of history. It is not, as commonly understood, scientific; though this does not deny the possibility of balance.

[2] That is not to say that either the Church, in the past, or the media or education today simply and always reproduces the interests of the ruling class. (e) Class struggle defines what the ruling class can get away with. At the end of the second world war, the ruling class was weak, millions had died for a better more just world. Significantly, large numbers of workers were armed, there were radical alternative ideologies. In this context huge gains were made for the working class in housing, benefits, social security, education and health. However, since 1948 those gains have been rolled back because of neo-liberalism and the weakness of the labour movement today.

[3] It is this largely ideological role of the state that creates what Marx calls 'false consciousness' we believe that there is no alternative that the way we do things are natural are in accord with human nature, so we are told competition is natural, the free market is inevitable. Yet, we know that humans cooperate at least as much as they compete within families, within business, within nations. It is also apparent that the market is not free, but continually recreated as governments intervene to maintain 'competition' and the market. The logical result of competition is a winner, economically this is called monopoly the sole producer and evidenced through the domination of the corporations. Yet, the government will continue with the charade; corporations compete or tender to run our railways and utilities. Even worse our school system and health care are being wrecked through the ideological imposition of the

'free market'. Yet ideologies have been successfully challenged. Feminism opposed the 'natural role of women' as solely home cooks, cleaners and child carers as well as the innate superiority of men. Patriarchal ideology portrayed the oppressed role of women as natural, to challenge it was to go against nature. However, the women's movement successfully challenged that perception and few today would argue that women's only role is in the home. Similarly, the ideological instruments which mystifies capitalist reality can be challenged.

However, whilst the state can be relatively benign when the economy is buoyant, delivering a version of 'the good life' to most of the population, when profits are threatened, when the economy is in crisis, then the gloves come off. At these times the state control of the armed forces, the police, and the judicial system, often conspiring with the media, repress brutally the working class and their allies. (Orgreave/Belonging) This can be particularly vicious abroad; as in Argentina during the time of the 'disappeared', during the dictatorship in Chile or in South Africa post and pre-apartheid. In these instances, thousands have lost their lives. (f) Yet, in the past Britain, has been just as brutal witness Amritsar in India, the Peterloo Massacre but more recently Orgreave where the mounted police were unleashed against the picketing miners and the event reconstructed by the BBC to give the appearance of the miners as initiating the violence and the police restoring law and order. The BBC apologised for a mix up in the cutting room a year after the historic struggle of the NUM and its defeat. Finally, it would be remiss not to point out that men have not only used ideology to keep women 'in their place' but violence. Domestic violence is still widespread. Repressing women was achieved through a combination of ideology and violence. The ruling class use the same combination of ideology and repression. Indeed, the double edge sword of class dominance, as identified by Marx, still dominates our world as real freedom fighters continue to be incarcerated (g) and the vast numbers of our potential allies are divided through racism, sexism and elitism.

MAN MAKES RELIGION, RELIGION DOES NOT MAKE MAN

Whilst it was clear that religious teaching, ideas and beliefs could be used to justify the status quo it was equally possible to select ideas and beliefs which promoted the interests of the oppressed. Liberation theologists, such as Oscar Romero and Dom Hilda Camera (1) have sided with the poor in South America, Martin Luther King Jnr, a Christian, was a leader in the Civil Rights movement as was Malcom X, a Muslim. All based their resistance on their faith. Clearly, religion could be utilised to promote and inspire social change or to justify repression and maintain existing inequalities.

However, for Marxists "The mode of production of material life conditions the social, political and intellectual life process in general. It is not the consciousness of men that determines social being, but, on the contrary, their social being which determines consciousness" (Marx 1859, 503). It is not ideas descending from heaven that transforms the world but "real active men...on the basis of their real-life process" (Marx 1846, 47). Mankind as Engels stated at Marx's graveside "must first of all eat, drink, have shelter and clothing, before it can pursue politics, science, art, religion" (Engels, Frederick 1883). For Marx the important point is to explain the social basis of religion, to provide a materialist explanation. For Marx religions are merely distorted reflections and expressions of real social needs and interests. Consequently, from *'The peasant War in Germany'*

> In the so-called religious wars of the 16th century, very positive material class interests were at play, and those wars were class wars just as were later collisions in England and France.

And from *The History of Early Christianity*

> [The risings of peasants and plebeians in the Middle Ages], like all mass movements of the Middle Ages, were bound to wear the mask of religion and appeared as the restoration of early Christianity from spreading degeneration... But behind the religious exaltation there was every time a tangible worldly interest.

Consequently, as stated by the Marxist John Molyneux in 'More Than Opium: Marxism and religion' Oliver Cromwell the revolutionary and regicide in England became Cromwell the oppressor in Ireland.

Dutch Protestant burghers could be heroes of Europe in the Dutch Revolt but villains in Africa with apartheid. Any socialist looking at Ireland in the 1916 will identify with 'Catholic' nationalists not 'Protestant' Unionist. (Molyneux 2008)

Clearly, for Marx it is the social basis of religion we need to grasp; man makes religion, religion does not make man. Molyneux continues

> society produces, an inverted view of the world in which humans bow to an imaginary god of their own making, because it is an inverted world in which people are dominated by the products of their own labour...religion is not just a random collection of superstitious beliefs...it is the way in which alienated people try to make sense of their alienated lives and alien society.

As a result, Marxists do not insist workers become atheists or consider banning religion. The only sense in which Marxists contemplate the elimination of religion is through its gradual withering away due to the disappearance of its underlying social causes-alienation, exploitation, and oppression. For Marxists, according to Molyneux, the point of departure is not religious beliefs but rather the political role of the movement based on the social forces and interests which it represents.

Note

1. Archbishop Oscar Romero was assassinated on the 24th March 1980 in San Salvador. He spoke out against poverty, social injustice, assassination, and torture in El Salvador. Similarly, Dom Helder Pessoa Camara was a Brazilian Roman Catholic Archbishop who spoke out on behalf of the poor and the oppressed. He is famous for saying "When I give food to the poor they call me a saint.When I ask why the poor have no food, they call me a communist".

RELIGION AND ALIENATION

Grounding Religion in the material conditions of society and in the alienation suffered by humanity neatly explains both religion as a conservative force to justify the status quo and as an ideology of liberation. In neither case does the religion or beliefs or dogma mean anything of itself but rather the inverted projections of an alienated humanity and or the opportunistic, ideological veneer of class interests.

Religion, for Marxists, will wither away with the end of alienation and the maturing of socialism into communism. The verification of this projection lies in the future. However, basing early religion on alienation; on man's inability to control nature (Novak p66) or his environment has a rationale, but it can also be argued that though such 'alienation' decreased with humanity's increasing control over nature, so religion rather than diminish developed. Religious myths did not become less but more sophisticated in both their scope and interpretation.[1]

So Marxists now argue, that, with the onset of capitalist production, alienation mutates and becomes grounded in private property (Mandel/Novak p66) and the dominance of commodity production;

where the wage labourer is now separated from free access to the means of production (Mandel/Novack p20), itself a recent development in human history. In commodity production man becomes oppressed by his own creations rather than a lack of control over nature

> Miracles of God become superfluous because of the miracles of industry...the influence of unconquered nature as a factor in producing alienation is small compared to economic causes (Mandel/Novak p68).

Further,

> In capitalist society money has displaced religion as the major source of alienation... just as money has displaced the deity as the main object of adoration (Mandel/Novak p70)

It wouldn't be the first time that consumerism and materialism have been likened to religion or God. After all, the machinations of the market are little understood by most people, many of them economists! Perhaps market ideologies are the modern myths. Perhaps atheism is a 'religion' for modernity. What use is a 'god' in the jousting between egos as consumers or producers. Isn't it the survival of the fittest and damn the rest? Possibly for some, but the point is that however valid Marxist observations of religion maybe it is partial. Alienation may well contribute to our understanding of early religion, but it is not the whole story, not least because its 'explanatory' power is so elastic. It is teleological and still doesn't offer an explanation for the persistence and growth of religion within the context of global capitalism.

Marxism has grounded religion in alienation; initially, in man's lack of control over nature, but religion has persisted and evolved itself. The source of alienation is now rooted in commodity production, yet religion persists. True it has, at times, adapted according to the different interests of social classes and the hypocrisy between the expressed beliefs and human practice is revealing. Yet, for some Marxists these inconsistencies are easily explicable

> For a religion to become "major", that is to survive over centuries in many locations and different social orders, it is a precondition that its doctrines be capable of almost infinite selection, interpretation and adaption. Once again, what is decisive is not doctrine but social base in the specific social situation. (Molyneux 2008)

Yet, Marxism, itself is a set of ideas, revolutionary ideas granted, but still the product of social conditions. Marxists come in many hues with each 'sect' claiming to be the authentic voice of Marx. At times the practice of those who claim to be Marxist or Communist has horrified those who profess Marxism. Stalin's crimes were a cogent argument against communism yet Marxists, rightly in my opinion, argue that *authentic* Marxism continues to have a major, nay an indispensable, contribution to make to world history.

However, the reason the Marxist view of religion is partial, and consequently flawed, is because it focuses on an idealised, alienated concept of religion.

Just as formal logic focused its attention on the natural world and facilitated the growth and maturing of science, so dialectical materialism facilitated an understanding of the unfolding and development of human history. Enabled humanity to recognise their place in the world and the possibilities for making history. As Marx said in the 'The Eighteenth Brumaire of Louis Bonaparte "men make their own history ...but under circumstances existing already, given and transmitted from the past" (Marx 1852 p398). So, men make religion and indeed in circumstances they inherit, and have done so for millennia. However, they do so for a reason, a very practical reason, not based on some spurious relationship to alienation but for an intention that goes to the root of what we need to understand as religion. A logic focuses the mind on a particular area, with the appropriate logic or lens we can see what needs to be seen but without the right logic or lens what matters can be missed altogether. What is required is a logic that unmasks religion in its alienated idealised garb and for this we need to look at the work of John Macmurray.

Note

1. Ancient myths tend to reflect the culture and society which they represent so marauding Norsemen have Valhala the hall for slain warriors, where they feast under the leadership of their God Odin (Valhala 2018). Today Mathew Fox in 'One River, many Wells' brings together many different traditions and religions where people can share one another's spiritual riches and weave them into a common web that still values diversity and difference (Fox 2000).

JOHN MACMURRAY: MARXISM AND THE PERSONAL

Marx rejected idealism, the doctrine that ideas or thoughts make up reality. For Marx understood human society as an organic process and therefore understood dialectically (Macmurray 1933 October p19). 1 Indeed, "any social action which attempts to create reality in terms of an idea of what reality should be commits the fallacy of thinking that reality lies in the idea and not in the thing" (Macmurray 1933 October p43) For, "it is thought that must adapt itself to things...The thing will not accommodate itself to our idea of it. We have to change our ideas and keep on changing them until we get them right (Macmurray 1933 October p21) For example, miasma theory held that disease was caused by the presence in the air of miasma, a poisonous vapour. The germ theory of disease emerged in the second half of the 19th century and gradually replaced miasma theory (Wikipedia 1918). The idea had to accommodate to the 'thing' in this case the transmission of disease...but, continues Macmurray, there is something else besides 'the thing' which we contrast with thought and that is action...the moment we act we contact with things not ideas...action is primary, and thought is secondary" (Macmurray 1933 October p24-26). Indeed, it was through action that the miasma theory was challenged. As Marx famously quoted "Philosophers have only interpreted the world, in various ways; the point is to change it" (Marx 1846). Indeed, as we do ourselves. "We are society and to refashion society is to remake ourselves" (Macmurray 1933 October p43)

Similarly, if people want to know what a political party really stands for they study what it does when in power. Not necessarily what it proclaims about itself. Clearly, what people are looking for "is that our ideals and practice should be in agreement" (Macmurray 1933 October p41); this is what we find with experimental science where all theories are tested by action and ultimately how all non-idealist theory requires to be judged, including religion.

For Macmurray the development of society is measured by the change in the form of human relationships. If we wish to understand this process, we have to decide what it is that governs the change in the social relationships of persons in society (Macmurray 1933 October p46). Indeed, for Macmurray, it is persons in relation that are the substance of society.

> When we talk as economists of the relation of capital and labour, we are apt to forget that capital and labour are ideas not

things...Therefore the relation between capital and labour really means the relationship between people who won't starve if they don't work and the people who will starve if they don't work. Until you get down to the relationship between people, you haven't reached the reality of the thing you are talking about...if we want to understand the present crisis we have to understand it not in terms of trade returns or movement of prices, but in terms of starvation, ill health and quite personal changes. 2

John Macmurray was writing, in this instance, during the depression in the 1930s. It is as true today in our times of austerity. Marx also talks of person's in relation but in this case as defining your class. Yet, even human relations are of more than one type. First there are relations where one is an instrument for another. Yet, others where people cooperate for the achievement of a common purpose. Both these relationships can be understood with dialectical materialism; as Marx does with his analysis of history through class conflict. However, a third type of relation consists of the relationship of person to person. This type of relationship, friendship, is found within any period of social development. "Friendship is just friendship in England or equatorial Africa, in the twentieth century AD or in the twentieth century BC". (Macmurray 1933 October p66) Such relationships Macmurray calls personal and cannot be interpreted in mechanical or organic terms. They are essentially ultimate expressions of human nature, they constitute the social aspect of what distinguished human life from merely organic life. (Macmurray 1933 October p66) Macmurray characterises the personal as Superorganic. The principle being that an organic process is inadequate to understand personal experience. For, Macmurray, friendship is only possible on the basis of equality and is always mutual and intentional. (Macmurray 1945). It is also central to Macmurray's understanding of religion. Indeed, for Macmurray religion is about personal relationship.

Clearly, for Macmurray, the personal is universal, across all ages and all cultures. Its essential nature is only understood through immediate experience (Macmurray 1933 March p124). Neither can personal relationship be abstracted, as the relationship is essential to the situation being reflected upon. Whatever that may be. Indeed, for Macmurray "we know persons only by entering into personal relationship with them as equals". In addition, and as a corollary, it

> rests upon the recognition that whenever one person treats another as an instrument for his use as an object for his enjoyment, he denies in practice-which is more important

> than theory- the others essential nature as a
> person. (Macmurray 1933 March p126) (simi-
> lar to Marx and appendage to a machine)

Indeed, the self exists only in the communion of other selves. 'I' exists only as one member of the 'you and I'. My own experience as a person is constituted by my knowledge of other persons. I am 'I' because I know you, and you are you because you know me; it is my knowledge of other persons and not the mere fact of relationship; (Macmurray 1933 March p137) and each of us can only be one 'I'. The other person is always 'you'. Also, I know that for yourself you are 'I' and to you I am the other 'you'. So, it is also each person's otherness which is essential to their individuality. (Macmurray 1933 March p139).

These relationships cannot be represented mathematically for which all units are equally 'it'. Organic thought can represent essential differences between elements in a whole, but this is in terms of a complementary function (Bourgeoisie/proletariat) no element in an organic whole can be really individual. (Macmurray 1933 p139).

The personal involves the essential individuality of all persons as well as their differences. It is as a personal being that all knowledge and all that is experienced is taken up. Indeed, it is only through the personal that I can be rational and know the world. For Macmurray, this immediate experience of the personal, through the community of conscious beings, is to touch the experience of the infinite personality in finite individuals. The experience of the personal absolute, as the unity of persons in relationship, is, for want of a better word, the experience of God. (Macmurray 1933 March p138) 3

Now this is not idealist, as its rationale is grounded in action and people as they are. It is, I think, worth sticking with the word God as it points to something real that is larger than our own individuality whilst itself being grounded in that individuality as friendship. In this way our understanding of religion itself evolves.

Further, there doesn't have to be anything unreal about the continuity of life itself, once the ego is taken out of it. The cycle of birth, life and death goes on. However, it may be argued that the notion of 'God', suggested above, is simply a projection. Personally, I don't think so, but this can be debated, and people can adopt the 'best fit theory' the one that works for now. It is not the idea that is central but rather what we do that counts. Religion is tested not by the wisdom or truth of our belief but how we live our lives. For me love reflects our real nature and can only be expressed in a relationship. To be fully human is to love one another. To love one another is what good religion requires of each one of us, alongside forgiveness and to do unto others as you would be done by. These are the lubricants of a good society, a real working community.

Notes

1.Marx's dialectical interpretation of human history and economics is principally adequate as society adapts itself to its environment. The environment does not adapt society to itself. The governing factor is merely to say that society must adapt itself to material conditions of life if it is not to perish. However, man has also attempted to adapt the environment to man by understanding and controlling the laws of nature. It is understanding natural laws, that of themselves make it impossible for humans to fly, that human beings became able to construct machines in which they can fly. In this respect the economic interpretation of history is only applicable to the immaturity of social life. However, in proportion to humanity's control over nature human development ceases to be merely an organic process and becomes Superorganic(More later!). Conversely, so long as the development of society is not rationally understood it remains an organic process.

2. Institutions are not real they are reifications and seem real, they are the apprehension of human phenomena as if they were things. It is the people in them and outside them that are real; though clearly institutions do have real effects on people such as the banks, mortgage loans, interest rates. Yet, they are all human creations even if they regularly have us chasing our tails.

3. God is the term which symbolises the infinite apprehended as personal, and it derives, as indeed, it must from our immediate experience as finite persons. The idea of incarnation, which in one form or other appears in all immediate religions, merely expresses the fact that our awareness of the personal infinite comes to us, and can only come, in and through our awareness of finite personality (Macmurray 1933 March p124). Of course, God is beyond the personal but it is the personal in our experi-

Jonathan Smith

ence which points in the direction of God... and provides the
most adequate language we possess for references to God

GOOD RELIGION, BAD RELIGION

Religion is not simply about cherry picking beliefs but rather looking at what religion does, what works, what is the good society? Indeed, the idea 'heaven on earth' is a way of perceiving a world where freedom and justice meet, and the bread of life is shared more equitably. It is a religious aspiration. Yet, how can it be achieved and how do we know when we are on the right road? To go some way in answering the last question is to reflect upon the scientific method. Just as science developed theories to control the natural world and discards those that are falsified, that don't work so with religion it is important to discard those aspects that don't work. For example, literal quotes from holy books which reflect patriarchal nonsense about the role of women or the creation of the universe are completely idealist and detract from embedded wisdom as rational people can no longer take it seriously.

Indeed, for Macmurray scientific scrutiny destroyed religions dogmatic claims. (Macmurray 1965 p14) His own religious world view, as a practicing Scottish Presbyterian, had been shattered by the First World war. At the onset of war, the European

Churches, for the most part, rallied behind their perceived and respective national interests. Clearly, the Churches did not mean what they said; love your enemies, forgiveness, do unto other as you would be done by. This was a moral not an intellectual problem. From that moment, for Macmurray, Christianity had to be rediscovered and recreated. (Macmurray 1965 p22).

In the 1930s Macmurray attended a private conference which had one agenda item 'What is Christianity?'. The participants concluded that to answer the question it was essential to study two questions. First, the nature of Communism and the other the problem of sex (Macmurray 1965 p25) 1. This led Macmurray, in addressing the first question, to research the early writings of Karl Marx. (Macmurray 1965 p25).

Marx had rejected religion as the popular form of idealism and Macmurray agreed that idealism is a dangerous illusion, but that religion was not necessarily idealist. (Macmurray 1965 p26). Indeed, Christianity had only become idealised with the acceptance of the Roman Empire. Christianity became aligned with the Roman state, acquiesced to the artificial separation of temporal and spiritual worlds as well as institutionalising parallel hierarchical and authoritarian structures that remain central to the major Christian religions of today. Macmurray argued that, a purely spiritual religion is an idealist religion and so unreal and it led him to speculate that "Communism might well be that half of Christianity which had been dropped by the Church in favour of an accommodation with Rome". (Macmurray 1965 p27)

For real religion is about community; for the ancients the common ceremonial experience created a sense of belonging with the dead, the living and the unborn. It created a tribal unity (Macmurray 1965 p31). Rituals accompanied agriculture but for the ancients these were not separate from the process of cultivation they were all of a piece and their wholeness is religious (Macmurray 1965 p33). The forces of nature are *personal* forces for the ancients. Consequently, Macmurray regards community, the relationship between human beings and the world and between person and person, as permanent and central features of religion. Further, whilst immature man had an immature conception of the divine there is, nevertheless, a sense of something more in our experience which is somehow personal, which transcends our familiar experience of life in common, and yet which faces us when we reflect deeply upon our everyday activities. (Macmurray 1965 p34).

However, primitive religion is limited to a finite group, the tribe or nation. On the other hand, a mature religion is universal with a corresponding universal brotherhood. Unfortunately, as yet, there is clearly no universal brotherhood. Indeed, mankind is split up into a collection of peoples and nations, this disunity of humanity is a failure, a tragedy for in our religious life as we ought to be a single community. (Macmurray 1965 p38) This is the essential rational for the significance of the personal. Any two people in the world can be friends. Can love one another. Friendship is a spiritual relationship. It is transcendental, it is more than class, gender, age or ethnicity and even species.

In primitive religion the extension of a limited group was achieved through the ritual pretence of a blood-relationship, today that is a nonsense, but nevertheless the problem, the reality of universal brotherhood remains practical and will only be resolved through action. It cannot be resolved through thinking or emotional attachment to ideas. Neither can it be forced, you cannot make people love one another. (Macmurray 1965 p39)

Consequently, good religion is concerned with reality now, with action and with community, with people in personal relationships (Macmurray 1965 p59). Idealism or bad religion seeks to escape action and community by focusing on an ideal 'the hereafter' or beliefs which have no correspondence with reality. When the primary focus of Christianity or religion becomes to save 'my soul' it has become idealised or at best, an insurance policy for dealing with our own physical mortality. However, our mortality is shared, a common experience, which can help to unify us rather than divide us into those who believe one thing rather than another and has the rest of us damned. 2

Religion is for the sake of the world, not for the benefit of the worshipper. Further, "The material life is the spirit in practical expression... Consequently, what a man believes is expressed in his way of life. If what he professes... differs...then he is either mistaken about what he believes, or he is hypocritical" (Macmurray 1965 p65). Clearly, what makes us Christians, or religious, is an attitude of mind and a way of life, how we treat each other...and that is a sufficient basis of unity. As John Macmurray emphasises the effect of this is to shift the expression of religion from theory to practice. "By their fruits ye shall know them" becomes the accepted rule (Macmurray 1965 p70). It would have the advantage of showing how divergent views and doctrines could be held within a unity of love and avoid definitive doctrines or binding orthodoxies which simply divide. (Macmurray 1965 p70)

Our humanity lies in our relations to other human beings and in the quality of these relations. Likewise, "our relation to God is itself real only as it shows itself in our relation to our neighbours". (Macmurray 1965 p72). Indeed, following this "we might create a new and acceptable kind of theology, which should be undogmatic and which like modern science, would recognise the hypothetical and temporary character of all its findings… empirical in temper… and freely critical of the past." (Macmurray 1965 p73).

Indeed, religious groups should have no authority save the authority of love. Freedom, equality and brotherhood are religious ends. Thus, declares Macmurray, to think that the disparity of material resources between rich and poor need make no difference to community or communion is disingenuous. (Macmurray 1965 p78)

Notes

1. John Macmurray discusses religion with reference to Christianity and it is Christianity that has monopolised, until recently, faith in Western Europe. It is part of the cultural heritage. I know something of Christianity but little of the other major religions. I would hope, in the future, to be able to reference other faiths more fully. I am involved in interfaith projects but feel inadequate, for the present, to make any confident assertions.

2. In the Creative Society John Macmurray doesn't mince his words "so long as a religious doctrine of immortality is taken to signify the unreality of death, it is the devils work" (Macmurray 1935 p50)

PERSONAL LOGIC: THE SELF AND PERSONS IN RELATION

Macmurray argues that only by becoming authentically religious can a person be fully rational, and objective in feeling thought and action. (Macmurray 1991 p x). How he comes to this conclusion is by a rejection of the primacy of theory over action. Indeed, "to adopt the standpoint of action is not to exchange one theory for another but to change the basis of all theory" (Macmurray 1991 p xvii). It is to look at the world afresh. Like Marx's dictum that philosophers have only interpreted the world, but the point is to change it. The focus is on action. This requires a shift from our concern with the self which, with modern philosophy based on Descartes's dictum 'I think therefore I am', is largely egocentric (Macmurray 1991 p35). 1. The self cannot exist, as it is a logical abstraction, and can only exist in a community of personal agents. (Macmurray 1991 p12). The purely individual self is pure fiction. (Macmurray 1991 p38). Further, by adopting the 'I think' as a starting point makes it impossible to do justice to the religious experience as the 'Self' is already committed to individualism and fails to allow for knowledge of you and I, of the unity of one another. (Macmurray 1991 p71) Consequently, for Macmurray a "new phase of philosophy would rest on the assertion that the self is neither substance or an organism but a person" (Macmurray 1991 p37). 2 Significantly, just as a substance can be derived from the organic so the organic can be derived from the person but the process cannot be reversed. Only persons know and act with knowledge. (Macmurray 1991 p126). 3

Macmurray also makes an important distinction between an event and an action. The former has a cause-a formal logical expression- whilst an action has a reason- a personal logical expression. For action is intentional and can only be understood with reference to the purpose of a person. (Macmurray 1991 p150). No person can compel another person, at most they can provide motive for another's desired action (Macmurray 1991 p154). However, the motive may be negative or positive, that is it may be promoted through fear or love. (Macmurray 1999 p99) Further, only spontaneous initiation of change is the act of a person as agent, whilst habit is the negative aspect of action, without which action could not itself take place. It reflects those actions which have been learned based upon prior intentions. Indeed, all human action is grounded in intention. A person or animal may be motivated to act out of fear but the act a person performs is determined by intention whilst the "fear felt by an animal completely determines its behaviour, fear felt by a human does not. Fear, like love, can be acted out in many ways" (Macmurray 1991 p xxi). (Macmurray 1991 p162). 4 Consequently, simple action is incomplete, for 'I do' in actual experience means 'I am doing this and not that' (Macmurray 1991 p165).

The primacy of action, of people as agents, necessarily means that any theory which implies that the world is fully determined is false. (Macmurray 1991 p127). 5 Indeed, any antinomy between freedom and determinism vanishes with agent, with people in action; for to possess free will is simply to be able to determine the indeterminate, that is the future. (Macmurray 1991 p134). As an agent, as a person acting in the world, the present is determined for me. What has been done cannot be undone. It is only in the here and now that action can take place. I can act neither in the past or the future. However, in determining the future a person determines an environment which itself provides a limitation to future action. (Macmurray 1991 p135-139). 6

Further, action is always directed by an awareness of the Other; which, if more than a reaction to a stimulus, requires knowledge of the Other. Such knowledge is achieved through reflection, itself conditioned, by selectivity of attention and a withdrawal from action. (Macmurray 1991 p168-173). Reflection is always about the past, it is retrospective whereas what is intended is always about the future; and whilst there are no future facts, it may, of course, be that something anticipated will in fact happen. (Macmurray 1999 p39) Yet, reflection is also incomplete until it is expressed, and this can take three forms; religion, art and science. Religion is inclusive as the other two are defined by a limitation of attention.

To make this clear, consider the beginning and end of an act, both are defined by a person's feeling; either as a feeling of dissatisfaction or satisfaction. In this sense emotional reflection is primary. (Macmurray p194) Indeed, valuation is the vanguard of any action governed by intention. However, when this is limited to intellectual understanding, to understanding the world as means or, more simply, how we do something, then, if carried out systematically, it is science. Science is instrumental knowledge limited to the technical field. It permits of no explanation through intention or purpose (Macmurray 1961 p19-21). 7 On the other hand, if valuation is expressed as an end, for its own sake, and cannot be experienced in action then it is pure art. Consequently, scientific reflection aims at knowing everything in general but nothing in particular and knows a great deal about things without truly 'knowing' them. 8 (Macmurray 1991 p199). Whereas, art seeks to know about things in particular.

On the other hand, religion is inclusive as it is the audacious attempt to understand the world as a whole.

Religion aims at universality; even though, and unfortunately, the multiplicity of religion is clearly an indication of religions' current failure (Macmurray 1961 p8). Consequently, science resolves the means, how we achieve an objective or intention, and art addresses the ends, what it is intended. Whereas, the focus of religion embraces all of this and is achieved through community.

For science, art and religion are things that people do (Macmurray 1961 p29). We are clearly not isolated, and we cannot simply do or act as we please. Action depends upon personal relationships and it is this problematic from which religion derives. Indeed, it is the problematic of community which gives rise to religion. For example, its concern for reconciliation, is itself reflected in language used such as 'forgiveness and 'compassion' which clearly enable communities to persist. Consequently, the real meaning of religion, as opposed to an idealist reflection, can only be unambiguously expressed in action; with how we treat each other (Macmurray 1961 p52-57).

To conclude this section the intention is to identify how a consideration of personal relationships leads to a feeling for God. History is clearly one and every new history of an age is a rewriting of the one history. Indeed, the ideal of history can be considered to represent the whole human past as if it were the memory of a single agent. Nevertheless, what is actually recalled, is generally selected for its relevance to the present (Macmurray 1961 p207-212). Yet, this does not have to affect its validity as the co-operative process of reflection moves gradually towards a single, reliable and complete record of human activity in the past. However, neither is history a mere chronicle, it is understanding the continuity of the past with the present. Significantly, this can only be understood through the activity of human agents and as such can only be a continuity of action and thus intention (Macmurray 1991 p212-213). Now, whilst the person includes an organic aspect we are not just an organism, or even essentially an organism, we are persons. There is no social evolution only history; with both progress and regression. For, human behaviour is simply caricatured if it is represented as an adaptation to the environment. (Macmurray 1999 p46)

Unfortunately, much of contemporary thought conceives the world as a single process; either biologically as an evolutionary process or mathematically as a material process of events obeying physical laws; it is the direction of such thought that promotes an atheistic conclusion. However, these conceptions are an abstraction from our experience as agents, as people. For, such understanding excludes action. Neither, should it be suggested, can it be said that all actions are determined, for the capacity to act is freedom. Consequently, once we accept the primacy of action then, in turn, the argument points towards a belief in the reality we call God. For to think the world in practical terms is ultimately to think of the unity of the world as one action, and therefore informed by a unifying intention. (Macmurray 1991 p221)

Clearly, what is understood as religion has changed. No longer need it be idealist and locked into beliefs validated by tradition. Faith does not mean to believe the unbelievable rather to have faith is to have courage to act to make universal love real. The locus for conceiving the world as personal is to open ourselves to God. The transition from 'I think' to 'I do' drives us to conceive of a personal universe in which God is the ultimate reality in which the universe is fully intended; whilst remembering that religious doctrines are as problematic as scientific theories and require constant revision and verification in action by persons who are prepared to commit themselves intentionally to the way of life which they proscribe (Macmurray 1999 p223) 9

Notes

1. The more modern philosophy claims to be purely objective the more inevitable atheism (Macmurray 1991 p19)

2. So long as our most adequate concept is the organic concept our social planning can only realistically issue in a totalitarian society (Macmurray 1991 p83)

55

3. In seems Marx substituted the self 'as a thinker' for self as 'a worker' and work, like thinking is only one of the things we do.

4. Macmurray regards habit in human behaviour replacing instinct in animal behaviour with the further proviso that what can be learned can be unlearned (Macmurray 1999 p53).You only need imagine any action you undertake which necessarily implies many other actions which are not currently intentional but the result of habit, it is not an organic motive as they are not innate but have to be learned.

5. This is true of any Marxism that regards socialism and communism as inevitable.

6. Marx recognises this in the Germany Ideology stating that 'men make history albeit in circumstances which they inherit', though his assertion is organic and removed from the person with choice and intention.

7. The intention to make a bomb is value the how to is not.

8. An engineer can know all there is about how an engine works but the good mechanic will 'know' the engine in ways the theoretical model does not allow. Indeed, people readily say talk about the significance of getting a feel for a particular engine or car.

9. It is important, at this point, to dispel the dualistic notion that judgments of value are simply emotive and cannot be true or false. Those who assume that only judgments of facts can constitute knowledge as they have objective meaning which permits verification, neglect that this doctrine is itself a valuation. If thoughts are verified in action so are valuations. An assertion of fact is an expression of my thought just as an assertion of value is an expression of emotion. If it can be an incorrect or correct description of an object why may not the expression of a feeling for an object be a correct or incorrect valuation of an object? Both seek to make other people think as I do. The only relevant difference is that to verify a valuation I must commit myself inaction toward making it my end. An experiment that may well cost you your life. (Macmurray 1991 p202)

MARXISM AND PERSONS
IN RELATION

Writing between the two World Wars Macmurray, with the then limited knowledge of the reality in Stalinist Russia, regarded the social experiment in Soviet Russia as the

> Nearest approach to the realisation of the Christian intention that the World has yet seen, for the intention of a universal community based on equality and freedom, overriding differences of nationality, race, sex and "religion", is its explicit and conscious purpose. (Macmurray 1938 p206)

Yet, he regarded both Bolshevism and Fascism as the two ideals which rest upon the "deification of organised society. Both of them believe...that a man's whole goodness consists in being a good citizen". (Macmurray 1932 p148) he goes on to say of the two I would choose Bolshevism before stating

> But I don't want either. I believe that a man's goodness consists in being a man in all the fullness of his humanity; and for that he must be free. A man's true significance does not lie in his job... it lies in being a

man-in the quality of his own consciousness.
There have been men who died rather than
deny the integrity of their own humanity,
and they are the moral heroes of the world.
(Macmurray 1932 p148)

For Macmurray communism was and is unconscious
of its historic continuity with its Christian origin.
So, following the revolution in 1917 Russia was
communist in intention but not in fact. For the uni-
fication of theory and practice of the intellect and
emotion in communal life is the essence of religion.
The anti-religious mind looks to the state for solutions reducing the personal to an 'individual' matter. (Macmurray 1938 p207-209) Whilst, in reality,
"human society can only rest upon the acceptance of
all individuals of the communal nature of their own
personal lives" (Macmurray 1938 p209). In essence

The human issues of personal relationships are the centre of the whole process and
core of all human reality. If we limit our intention to the political life and economic aspects of life we shall lose our perspective.
1(Macmurray 1938 p219)

Clearly, Macmurray champions the logic of the personal but also went on to admonish Marx for his
cavalier treatment of religion

Marx's criticism of religion...is unscientific...
Religion is a device, he thinks, for taking

men's minds off their present miseries. It diverts their attention from this life to another and attaches their hopes to a world beyond. So, they are reconciled to their present lot and discouraged from any attempt to better it. It is 'opium for the people'; a promise of 'pie in the sky when you die'. It is the popular and therefore the effective form of idealism. How did he arrive at this theory? Was it by careful, objective study of the great variety of religions...There is no record of such study. When the hypothesis formed itself in his mind, did he seek to verify it by finding whether it would square with all the available evidence? Obviously not. If he had, he would surely have asked himself whether it accounted for the religion of his own Jewish ancestors as it is expressed in the Old testament literature. This would have been enough to disprove the hypothesis, or at least to require a drastic revision. For that religion at least is not idealistic, in Marx's sense but materialist. It shows no interest in any other world but is entirely concerned with the right way to maintain a community in this world. That some expressions of some form of religion are liable to his criticism...may hold, even of official Christianity in Western Europe in modern times. That would provide good ground for demanding

religious reform. But to make it the basis of
a theory of religion as such...is most unscientific. (Macmurray 1999 p153-154)

Macmurray goes on to identify the essential charac-
teristics of religion. First its universality, no society
has yet existed without a religion of some kind sig-
nifying that the source of religion must lie in common human experience. 2 Second, whilst there are
analogies of artistic, technological, or social aspects
of animal life there is no parallel with religion in
even the highest form of animal life. Third, religion
as a matter of historical fact has been the initial re-
pository of human reflection and expression of art
and science even though they are now autonomous.
Fourthly, religion is, in intention, inclusive of all
members. If they no longer *must* be members, they
ought to be. It is inclusive and universal and unlike
art or science does not require special talents from
its practitioners. (Macmurray 1999 p156-157)

For Macmurray, religion is about the basic formal
problem of human existence, and this is the relation of persons which if united by a common life
becomes a community, a group which acts together
in fellowship; this contrasts with a mere society
which only acts together to achieve a common end
where each member has a function united only in
common purpose. A community, on the other hand,
is maintained by mutual affection, each member of
the group is in positive relation to each other, there

is also a consciousness of the common life. However, this consciousness may not be realized, hostility make take the place of fellowship and is characteristic if personal relations become negatively motivated, if fear of others replace love of others. Thus, the problem of community is the problem of overcoming fear, and religion is the reflective activity which expresses the consciousness of community through the celebration of communion. (Macmurray 1999 p157-161) The fear is always of the 'other'. Yet, if we are, adopting Christian terminology, united in Christ then there is no ground for fear. 3 However, the further challenge for communities today, both within communities and between communities, is the coming together of different faiths. The significance of interfaith practice cannot be underestimated. The main stumbling blocks are those who claim an exclusive truth, usually written in scripture, which defines those who are in and excludes those who are out. As seen above religion is partial if not universal. So, religion now either reconstructs itself to become inclusive or destructs itself through conflict.

Religious ritual helps to forge and symbolise communion which in turn strengthens community. One aspect of this is the need for a person at its head, not for a ruler, but a ritual head, a representative of the unity of the community as a personal reality. This works within a culture or faith, say through a

priest, an imam, a rabbi but again can fracture between different cultures or different faiths. Yet, the
foundation of all faiths points to the reality we call
God, a personal God, as the universal personal Other.
Important, for God is larger than each of us and is not
parochial, political, or partisan. 4 All are loved. It
is totally inclusive; a problem only arises when cultures or faiths make God too little and claim 'God'
for themselves. 5

However, there are encouraging developments towards unity. Indeed, Mathew Fox in 'One River
Many Wells' has observed that religion can develop
its own institutional ego, even while preaching the
need to individuals to humble personal egos. For
Fox, there is a need to go to the core of human
religious traditions where there is really one experience expressed variously and with great diversity (Fox 2000 p2-3). Nicholas of Cusa, a scientist,
mystic and cardinal of the Roman Catholic Church
in the fifteenth century wrote "Even though you are
designated in terms of different religions, yet...in all
this diversity" there is "one religion". (Fox 2000 p3).
More recently, the Buddhist monk Thich Nhat Hanh
claims what is central "is not a matter of faith; it
is a matter of practice" (Fox 2000 p4). Once again,
it is what we do not what we believe. Father Bede
Griffiths, a Benedictine monk who lived for half a
century in India recognised that "If one starts with
doctrines, the arguments are endless...But when one

comes to the level of interior experience...is where the meeting takes place" (Fox 2000 p4). For surely, while we want to honour the differences between faiths, it is time to emphasize the likenesses, or what Griffiths calls "the universal religious tradition of mankind". (Fox 2000 p9) For, as Meister Eckhart put it "All paths lead to God, for God is on them equally for the person who knows".

Karen Armstrong won the 2007 TED prize for people who have made a difference. The recipient is given $100,000. At the award ceremony in February 2008 Karen asked TED to help launch a Charter for Compassion

> All faiths insist that compassion is the test of true spirituality and that it brings us into relation with the transcendence we call God, Brahman, Nirvana or Dao. Each has formulated its own version of what is sometimes called the Golden Rule: 'Do not treat others as you would not like them to treat you' – or in its positive form: 'Always treat others as you would wish to be treated yourself'. (Armstrong 2011 p1-2)

Thousands, internationally, contributed to the draft charter, then a group of notables from Judaism, Christianity, Islam, Hinduism, Buddhism and Confucianism met in February 2009 to compose the final version. 6 It has since been translated into over thirty different languages.

Such developments point to the potential for reconstructing our religious outlook into a powerful tool for change. For it is part of the evolutionary process but one that is clearly a choice. For, whilst we have inherited a reptilian brain that puts the ego first and as Karen Armstrong acknowledges

> We doubtless learned to run and jump in order to escape from our predators, but from these basic skills we developed ballet and gymnastics: after years of dedicated practice men and women acquire the ability to move with unearthly grace and achieve physical feats that are impossible for an untrained body. We devised language to improve communications and now we have poetry, which pushes speech into another dimension. In the same way those who have persistently trained themselves in the art of compassion manifest new capacities in the human heart and mind. (Armstrong 2011 p17-18)

It is not my intention, and certainly beyond my capacities, to map out the details for the road ahead. Rather, it is to point to the potential significance of religion in bringing us together rather than divide us. For it has always been the potential for religion when understood from a nondual perspective. 7 Indeed, many Christians today are recovering Contemplative practice and prayer "which teaches you not to make so much of the differences, but to return to who you are beyond your nationality, skin colour, gender, or other labels" (Daily Meditations October 18, 2015). For contemplation is more about changing ourselves and beginning to see through a nondual lens.

The remainder of this section looks at a selection from 'Daily Meditations' by Richard Rohr(Centerfor-ActionandContemplation meditations@cac.org) as one step towards looking at ourselves so we can more effectively engage with the world for meaningful change.

Cynthia Bourgeault observes that we begin "to discover that our Buddhist and Jewish and Islamic and Hindu friends are not competitors. Religion is not survival of the fittest. There is a deep understanding that we all swim or sink together. Each religious tradition reveals a colour of the heart of God that is precious" (Daily Meditations November 22, 2016)

Dom Helder Camara (famous for saying that 'When I give food to the poor they call me a saint. When I ask why they are poor, they call me a communist') goes on to say we need to use the intelligence God has given each of us to see one another as brothers and sisters. Further, but significantly, "If you will live your religion, you will become different" (Daily Meditations October 2o, 2015). Foundationally, love is who we are... The great illusion we must all overcome is the illusion of separateness. (Daily Meditations December 27, 2015) Unhealthy economics and politics exist because, even as Christians we largely operate out of a worldview of scarcity whereas there is more than enough for our need though never enough for our greed. (Daily Meditations January 29,2016) Indeed, a capitalist worldview makes a virtue out of accumulation, consumption and collecting...we need more and more of everything except love-...a finally unworkable situation. (Daily Meditations February 19, 2016)

Those reconstructing religion from the bottom up recognise that "social justice is an integral part of evangelisation, a constitutive dimension of preaching Gospel...we cannot continue to think of salvation as a merely private matter. We are wasting out time trying to convert individuals without challenging corporate sin" (Daily Meditations July 8, 2016)

Separation of church and state is important to safeguard freedom of religion and ensure that governments are not dominated by a single religion's interests but that does not mean people of faith should not participate in politics. Indeed, Christians were at the forefront of political and justice movements to abolish slavery, support women's suffrage, protect civil rights (Daily Meditations July 8, 2018). However, challenging injustice requires us to change so we can practice what we preach. Richard Rohr met "many social activists who were doing excellent social analysis and advocating crucial justice issues but were not working from an energy of love except in their own minds. They were still living out their false self with the need to win, the need to look good, the attachment to superior, politically correct self-image. They might have the answer, but they are not themselves the answer. In fact, they were often part of the problem...Jesus and great spiritual teachers first emphasize transformation of consciousness and soul. Unless that happens, there is no lasting or grounded reform or revolution. When a subjugated people rise to power, they often become as controlling as their oppressor because the same demon of power has never been exorcised in them. (Daily Meditations May 8, 2016)

These are not prescriptions, they are for reflection and consideration before we return to action. Hypotheses to be verified in action through our daily living. The early Christian Church tried to live their faith. Several early writings illustrate the commitment to Jesus' teachings. The Didache, written around AD 90 says "share all things with your brother, and do not say they are your own. If you are sharers in what is imperishable, how much more in things which perish". It was even asked at the time 'Can a rich man be saved?' St. Clement concluded that it was not necessary to renounce all your worldly possessions to be a believer, but it is surely questionable and dangerous to be rich. This is not about making judgement but illustrating how people lived their belief, the only real verification. (Daily Meditations April 27, 2015) Christianity has changed with the times, the most significant in AD 313 when Christianity was legalised. Overnight the Church moved from the bottom to the top, literally from the catacombs to the basilicas. Once the Christian Church became the established religion of the empire it started reading the Gospel from the position of maintaining power and social order instead of the wisdom that Jesus revealed. (Daily Meditations April 28, 2015). Resurrecting and reconnecting with that wisdom and that of other faiths to create a universal understanding of love and compassion is the task before humanity today. So that religion can serve to unite us rather than divide. Indeed, to make universal communion a reality.

Notes

1. Never was a truer and more tragic word spoken. The true nature of Stalinism and the crimes of the Gulag were one of the most effective arguments levelled against communism. Not until the demise of Stalin and after his crimes condemned were alternative paths to power seriously debated and acted upon.

2. Religion in the Soviet Union and China were simply driven underground or festered and deformed through the cult of personality.

3. For Christianity, Christ is the eternal amalgam of matter and spirit as one. They hold and reveal one another. Wherever the human and the divine coexist, we have the Christ. Wherever the material and the spiritual coincide, we have the Christ. That includes the material world, the natural world, the animal world (including humans), and moves all the way to the elemental world, symbolized by bread and wine... You and I are living here in this ever-expanding universe. You and I are a part of this Christ Mystery without any choice on our part. We just are, whether we like it or not. It's nothing we have to consciously believe. It's first of all announcing an objective truth. But if we consciously take this mystery as our worldview, it will create immense joy and peace. It gives us significance and a sense of belonging as part of God's Great Work. We are no longer alienated from God, others, or the universe. Everything belongs. And it is pure, undeserved gift from the very beginning. Participating in Christ allows you to know that "I don't matter at all, and yet I matter intensely—at the same time!" That's the ultimate therapeutic healing. I'm just a little grain of sand in this giant, giant universe. I'm going to pass in a little while like everyone else will. But I'm also a child of God. I'm connected radically, inherently, intrinsically to the Center and to everything else. (Daily Meditations October 28, 2016)

4. More often in practice, when a person has stood to represent the Other, it has excluded as well as included. This is seen from the tribal leader to monarchy and divine right, to Presidents and dictators. Clearly, man alone is not large enough or inclusive of all being.

5. For, it is suggested, that God is never an object to be found or possessed as we find other objects, but rather the one who shares our own deepest subjectivity (Daily Meditations November 23, 2016). Rather, God is a mystery of relationship, and in its deep-

est form this relationship is called love. (Daily Meditations November 25, 2016)

6. The Charter for Compassion

The principle of compassion lies at the heart of all religious, ethical and spiritual traditions, calling us always to treat all others as we wish to be treated ourselves. Compassion impels us to work tirelessly to alleviate the suffering of our fellow creatures, to dethrone ourselves from the centre of our world and put another there, and to honour the inviolable sanctity of every single human being, treating everybody, without exception, with absolute justice, equity and respect.

It is also necessary in both public and private life to refrain consistently and empathically from inflicting pain. To act or speak violently out of spite, chauvinism, or self-interest, to impoverish, exploit or deny basic rights to anybody, and to incite hatred by denigrating others - even our enemies - is a denial of our common humanity. We acknowledge that we have failed to live compassionately and that some have even increased the sum of human misery in the name of religion.

We therefore call upon all men and women ~ to restore compassion to the centre of morality and religion ~ to return to the ancient principle that any interpretation of scripture that breeds violence, hatred or disdain is illegitimate ~ to ensure that youth are given accurate and respectful information about other traditions, religions and cultures ~ to encourage a positive appreciation of cultural and religious diversity ~ to cultivate an informed empathy with the suffering of all human beings, even those regarded as enemies.

We urgently need to make compassion a clear, luminous and dynamic force in our polarized world. Rooted in a principled determination to transcend selfishness, compassion can break down political, dogmatic, ideological and religious boundaries. Born of our deep interdependence, compassion is essential to human relationships and to a fulfilled humanity. It is the path to enlightenment, and indispensable to the creation of a just economy and a peaceful global community.

People are invited to join up to the Charter by following the link https://charterforcompassion.org/charter/charter-for-compassion-in-translation

7. Dualistic and Nondual Thinking

If we are trying to rebuild Christianity from the bottom up, we need to try to understand Jesus, the one who began it all (even though he probably never intended to start a new religion). I am convinced that Jesus was the first nondual religious teacher of the West, and one reason we have failed to understand so much of his teaching, much less follow it, is because we tried to understand it with dualistic minds. In his life and ministry, Jesus modelled and exemplified nonduality more than giving us any systematic teaching on it. Our inability to fully understand him and seriously follow him may be partly because we have not been taught how to see nondually ourselves. We thought highly of the "mind of Christ" but there was little practical knowledge of how to get there...I will try to shed some light on the meaning of dualistic and nondual thinking, because until you put on wide-lens nondual glasses you cannot see in any genuinely new way. You will just process any new ideas with your old operating system.

Dualistic thinking, or the "egoic operating system," as my friend and colleague Cynthia Bourgeault calls it, is our way of reading reality from the position of our private and small self. "What's in it for me?" "How will I look if I do this?" This is the ego's preferred way of seeing reality. It is the ordinary "hardware" of almost all Western people, even those who think of themselves as Christians. The church has neglected its central work of teaching prayer and contemplation, allowing the language of institutional religion itself to remain dualistic and largely argu-

71

mentative. We ended up confusing information with enlightenment, mind with soul, and thinking with experiencing—yet these are very different paths. The dualistic mind is essentially binary, either/or thinking. It knows by comparison, opposition, and differentiation. It uses descriptive words like good/evil, pretty/ugly, smart/stupid, not realizing there may be a hundred degrees between the two ends of each spectrum. Dualistic thinking works well for the sake of simplification and conversation, but not for the sake of truth or the immense subtlety of actual personal experience. Most of us settle for quick and easy answers instead of any deep perception, which we leave to poets, philosophers, and prophets. Yet depth and breadth of perception should be the primary arena for all authentic religion. How else could we possibly search for God? We do need the dualistic mind to function in practical life, however, and to do our work as a teacher, a nurse, a scientist, or an engineer. It's helpful and fully necessary as far as it goes, but it just doesn't go far enough. The dualistic mind cannot process things like infinity, mystery, God, grace, suffering, sexuality, death, or love; this is exactly why most people stumble over these very issues. The dualistic mind pulls everything down into some kind of tit-for-tat system of false choices and too-simple contraries, which is largely what "fast food religion" teaches, usually without even knowing it. Without the contemplative and converted mind— honest and humble perception—much religion is frankly dangerous. (Daily Meditations January 29, 2017)

A KINDER POLITICS AND
WHY IT MATTERS

There are several world religions many with different branches or sects; it would be an understatement to say that they don't always get on in the
real world. However, the last section identified both
reason and ways for religions to converge. Christianity, as I understand it, calls us to forgive, to do unto
others as we would be done to and to love one another, such commandments if truly meant and acted
upon would go a long way to facilitate real communion and community. If we move from an idealist
position where we judge and differentiate by what
people profess to believe rather than by what they
do, then there is the ground for interfaith practice
to progress and develop real communion. It seems
all religion, and this is why it matters, is about community; how we get on with each other, how we heal
differences and how we move forward. These are not
new ideas. What is new is the focus on 'I do' rather than 'I think' and the centrality of the personal;
that is the centrality of relationships between each
other, animals, nature, and the planet itself. The personal is who we are.

Fundamentalism, of whatever religion, is essentially grounded in fear in the need for certainty and security. Fundamentalism is also exclusive, and hopelessly dualistic, as the world is divided into the saved and the damned. 1 It is also one reason religion can be scapegoated as the problem rather than focusing on the material and economic routes of a conflict. 2. However, if we can make 'I do' rather than 'I think' our focus then, it seems to me and as Macmurray advocates, that all religious texts can be looked at as hypotheses for living and the rich wealth of wisdom teachers can be harnessed to create a genuine universal brotherhood. Blasphemy would or could become meaningless and redundant as the new focus is on the quality of our relationships rather than what we think or believe. Real religion, of course, is grounded in love and respect and is the context within which beliefs can be shared as hypotheses for living. I suspect that the Old Testament belief of an eye for an eye would not get past first base and I hope many other archaic practices would follow. 3

Religious doctrines refer to the facts of everyday experiences, so instead of arguing and quoting authorities, as authorities rather than guides, simply look at the relevant facts; the facts of our personal relationships to one another. Clearly, these include the universal human experiences of love and hatred; of enmity and reconciliation. Religion is the effort to understand and live by the universal laws of this personal world- the laws of friendship. Such facts set the problems for which religion seeks a solution; and they provide the practical field in which experimentally religious beliefs can be tested and improved. Like science religion stands or falls by its ability to provide solutions that are universally valid. So, its final vindication must be its ability to solve the problem of a universal community of all humankind. (Macmurray 1945)

However, for Marx, religion was a problem to be overcome; but would inevitably dissolve after the socialist revolution since, according to Marx, its material routes of alienation and oppression meant it was no longer necessary. Today, secularisation and the ruling class control of the mass media diminishes, for Marxists at least, the role of religion. Nevertheless, idealist religion remains a real problem. Free thought and freedom itself is suspended if the faithful must submit to certain beliefs and rituals rooted in a holy book and tradition. On the other hand, real religion, based on what you do and the personal, is grounded in both freedom and equality. For without freedom and equality there can be no genuine friendship and no genuine community.

Interestingly, it is friendship which resolves alienation not revolution. Alienation and its symptoms, loneliness, alcoholism, drug addiction and mental illness is a product of capitalism and friendship and community can go a long way to resolve them. Further, to affectively change society also requires an

understanding of the significance of real community, real religion and the personal not only to heal
alienation but enable real change to happen.

Religion can be a huge motivator. If it is authentic
it can enable progressive change to happen. Martin
Luther King, a Christian, was a giant of the civil
rights movement, Malcom X, a Muslim, was another.
Mahatma Gandhi, a champion of Indian independ-
ence and human rights, was a Hindu. Yet, it can also
be reactionary and oppressive. Religion can be used
to bolster values which are increasingly abhorred
such as imperialism, slavery and archaic or medieval
notions of how we should treat each other. Once,
we accept that religion is a work in progress, that
it struggles with questions that humanity has faced
since the dawn of time then clearly it is not a space
that should be ignored or dismissed. Certainly, not
vacated for the those without love to define.

If we can take our religion seriously then we can
stop hating and make the world a better place.
Gandhi is famous for saying "You must be the
change you want to see in the world" (Gandhi's Top
10 Fundamentals for Changing the World https://
www.positivityblog.com 2:55 12/4/18). Then if we
want a just world we must be just ourselves, if we
want people to listen to us we must listen to others.
If we want sincerity, then we must be sincere. This is
real religion based on what you do not just on what
you think or believe. That is not to detract from

the significance of religious works. Gandhi, as a practicing Hindu, will have been inspired by his reflective study and knowledge of Hindu scriptures such as the Vedas and Upanishads. His study and reflection contributed to his understanding of non-violence.

So, it has been that religion is central to humanity and that Marx's critique of religion is simply focused on idealist religion. That real religion focuses on the personal, on relationship rather than belief; on what you do rather than what you think. Real religion claims for a universal humanity and should be assessed on its ability to fulfil this promise. To consciously create a world community. This change in perspective can also initiate a move towards affective interfaith practice, away from conflict and towards an expanding community. Possibly, a unified religion: As beliefs become hypotheses and as working hypotheses are tested in practice. 4 This is the work of John Macmurray. 5

Macmurray has identified the logic of the personal. It provides the context, the religious framework, within which our politics should be practiced and assessed. I think few would dispute that the world would be a better place if people can love, respect, forgive and be at peace with one another. The logic of the personal provides the philosophical grounding which makes this more than wishful thinking.

First, the logic of the personal, and its application, identifies how real change is possible. Second, real religion helps dissolve opposition to change and finally it charts a way forward for humanity.

Marx, in applying materialist dialectics, provided a clear and unique understanding of how capitalism developed and how it is but one stage in human history. He identified how Capitalism was initially progressive pushing aside medievalism, promoting the franchise and increasing humanity's control over nature. Marxists have also demonstrated how the thirst for profit and markets fuelled imperialist wars, the destruction of the planet as well as the industrialised slaughter of millions.

Marx based historical change on class conflict. Specifically, the exploitation of the proletariat by the bourgeoisie. Such class conflict would propel the working class from a class 'in itself', defined by an economic relationship, to a class 'for itself' where, with the aid of the revolutionary party, the proletariat would develop a level of political consciousness where it would recognise itself as an exploited class and seek to take power. The ruling class would not give up its power to the democratic majority but fight to defend their privileges using the media to control ideas and democratic outcomes as well as the police and armed forces to put down democratic change. 6 Yet, if the revolution was not drowned in blood, then its success would advent socialism as a transition to a communist egalitarian society.

There have been few successful revolutions since

Marx wrote and those that have occurred have not followed the expectations of Marx or many of his followers. Dialectical logic is good at understanding the organic development of society but as humanity's control over nature increases and as the level of consciousness develops so the logic of the personal becomes increasingly significant. (Macmurray 1933 March p72) To ignore the logic of the personal is to disable the revolution at the moment of its greatest need. I suspect a bolshevism schooled in the logic of the personal would not have torn itself apart. Indeed, the rise of Stalinism demonstrates how man alone is not enough and how action predicated upon 'iron laws of history' leads to the Gulag. How we understand how each and everyone of us should be treated is not only the harbinger of a new society but also the foundation for its possibility. Only love can beget love. 7

However, the personal when consciously applied has enabled change to occur more peacefully. Witness the Good Friday agreement, sponsored by the now infamous Tony Blair, which not only brought peace to Northern Ireland but the unlikely friendship between Martin McGuiness and Ian Paisley two of the main antagonists. 8 The South African Truth and Reconciliation Commission established to help deal with what happened under apartheid could also have been inspired by the logic of the personal. Its limitations have not been the personal but its narrow focus and lack of progress in the post Mandela government. In 2014 Tutu stated that the commission was meant to be a beginning, not an end. (20 years after the TRC hearings South Africa's pain persists- Times LIVE https://www.timeslive.co.za, delivered by Google 14:10 7/5/18)

The logic of the personal and real religion also makes political sense at several different levels, all of which reduce the resolve to resist change.

Class conflict is essentially an economic relationship. It is important that what we hope to achieve in a fairer, more just, and more equal society is good not just for the oppressed but also the oppressor. Fear will only sharpen resistance. Love and forgiveness, sincerely felt, will make change that more inviting. Marx himself recognised that chains also shackled the bourgeoisie. They were tied to the need for profit and the exploitation of their fellow human beings. In the same way Patriarchal marriage stunted real love between men and women. Both were poorer for it.

During the Cuban revolution Batista's soldiers knew they would not generally be executed by the revolutionary guerrillas. Consequently, they were more likely to surrender, their resolve to resist was limited. Once captured they surrendered their arms and were sent back to their homes unless they could be persuaded to join the revolution. A wise decision at all levels, humane, politically astute, and important for building a future society.

More recently, with the rise and fall of UKIP. Hating people, or abusing people, in UKIP, however distasteful their views, was never going to change their mind. Standing up to people who preach hate or promote policies which inflame divisions in society is necessary but demonising them leaves them no way in which to change or recognise the fear which grounds so many reactionary beliefs. Immigration is a case in point. People with nothing being placed upon people with very little and being offered even less are not going to welcome very limited resources being spread ever more thinly. But there is no lack of wealth in this country, there is abundance, more than enough for everyone's need but not as, already cited, for everyone's greed. Yet, being treated with respect and love, particularly by those groups they attack, opens the possibility for further change. This is also true for all people in society whether in other parties or members of the public.

In the Labour Party real change has started. Thousands have joined the Party since the election of Jeremy Corbyn as leader, doubtless enthused by the hope of a more just society and a leader who is sincere and has validated his beliefs and values throughout his life. Recognising the logic of the personal and practicing a kinder politics is going to help the party to operate internally and reach out more effectively to everybody political and non-political. Treating people with respect is crucial. Anti-Semitism has dominated the headlines. It is wrong and needs to be challenged both home and abroad. Islamophobia is also wrong. That both in different ways have been weaponised is also wrong. The treatment of Palestinians by the Israeli government is wrong and also needs to be challenged for the sake of our common humanity. This list is far from exhaustive, but a Kinder politics underpinned by a respect for the logic of the personal, the foundation of a real religion provides both a compass and an anchor to help forge a labour party that people will want to join and stay in. After all a broad Church is a kind of community.

That may have been a good place to finish but it is not just about the Labour Party. John Macmurray at the end of the second world war in a BBC radio broadcast said

I think there is only one world, and that religion is about this actual world we live in: and about the common experience that we all have in it. I have come to think that a purely spiritual experience is just an imaginary experience; and that a purely material world would be a dead mechanism in which there would be no human beings and no human experience, where I differ from people who say much the same thing and call themselves materialists is, what was on both sides of the wall has come together and made a new and complete world. They seem to have left the wall standing; stayed on the material side of it and keep saying there is nothing on the other side. They often give me the impression that they are afraid to look over the wall in case they find something. When the wall is gone there is only one world – but it is a much bigger world...if the people of the whole world are united by political and economic bonds, but are not united in personal fellowship, then there can be no peace in the world; only mutual frustration, which threatens to break out into open war.

...A new civilisation has to be created- a world civilisation. The people of the world have to be united in one human fellowship. It cannot be done by political pacts or business contrivances. It cannot be done by science; because it is a religious task; and only religion, in the nature of things, can accomplish it (Macmurray 1945 p28-30)

When Macmurray broadcast this last program on Thursday 17th May 1945 Christianity was his focus; since then Britain has become a multi faith society, from a world perspective it always has been. He called for a new religious reformation. Indeed, for a 'religion that modern science need not be ashamed to serve' (Macmurray 1936 June) This may or may not, by pass the established faiths. I don't think it will, but we shall see. What we can do, as from now, is to apply what John Macmurray recognised as the summation of his philosophy. I think it works. I hope you do too. Think on it. Please. "All meaningful knowledge is for the sake of action, and all meaningful action is for the sake of friendship" (Macmurray 1991 p15).

Notes

1. The criticism is of idealist religion not necessarily all those who practice it. Many fundamentalist religions have organised support for poor people through shelters and foodbanks.

2. The conflict in Northern Ireland was portrayed as religious when its root cause lay with its colonial legacy.

3. Interestingly 'an eye for eye' was initially progressive when retribution was totally disproportionate. If a clan was wiped out for a slight or insult then an 'eye for eye' could be regarded as a welcome limitation!

4. This applies to all works treated at dogmas political and religious.

5. It is also complemented by the work of theologians such as Richard Rohr and his colleagues who have, completely independently, also identified relationship as the core of religion.

6. Unfortunately, history is littered with examples; for now, consider the British Miners strike of 1984 where the BBC manipulated coverage of protests at Orgreave, portrayed the miners as thugs rather than victims of police brutality only to claim after the defeat that there was a mix up in the cutting room. This had shown miners throwing bricks at the police followed by police on horse back seeking to regain control when in reality the police had first charged the miners who broke, ran

and grabbed anything to defend themselves. If that is too tender, consider the Peterloo Massacre 16th August 1819.

7.   Other what if arguments come to mind. What if the repre-sentatives of the Bolsheviks had not murdered the Romanovs or their actions condemned? I think the episode not only took away the moral high ground from the Bolsheviks but also undermined their ability to resist later internal outrages against the Bol-sheviks themselves.

8.   Apparently, images of the pair laughing and joking together earned them the nickname "The Chuckle Brother" 'How Martin McGuinness and Ian Paisley forged an unlikely friendship' Inde-pendent.ie Newsdesk. 21 March 2017 6:42 am.

9.   Interestingly Tony Blair, was influenced by John Macmurray's writings. Indeed, he wrote a brief forward to 'The Personal World John Macmurray on self and society. Selected and Introduced by Philip Conford; Floris Books 1996. Note the date is prior to his position as Prime Minister. I can see the link between Macmur-ray's philosophy and the Good Friday agreement but clearly none between that and the disastrous war in Iraq.

ACKNOWLEDGEMENTS

I cannot claim that anybody was pushing me to write this book. No such luck! However, neither would I have been motivated or sufficiently informed or challenged without friends. I would like to thank my good friend Maurice Bartley for our endless discussions on Christianity and for first introducing me to John Macmurray's writings. He had initially lent me 'Reason and Emotion' but I first opted for the shorter Swarthmore Lecture 'Search for Reality in Religion'. A good place to start. Since then, I have searched out John Macmurray's published writings and found...well, stimulating is probably an understatement. I later joined a discussion group hosted by Gordon Ferguson and held at The Quaker Meeting House in Sheffield. I find our monthly meetings extremely useful in clarifying my own views as well as my interpretation of John Macmurray. I thank all those who attend and for their contributions.

I would also like to thank Pauline Wheat-Bowen, Maurice and Ellen Bartley for reading an early draft, and for their comments and encouragement as well as Professor Julian Stern for taking the time to read a draft and make constructive comment. My partner

Tishi I also thank for reading through a paper she would never otherwise have picked up unless I had asked her to. The things we do for love! Her eye for grammar and punctuation I hope have rendered my efforts readable. Finally, I would like to thank Max. Who said nothing, well nothing in English anyway, as he's a dog. A beautiful, slightly large roan Cocker Spaniel. Our daily walks provided those opportunities for reflection and inspiration, those moments when connections are made.

REFERENCE LIST

We are religious beings

Gray J (2016) *Why humans find it hard to do away with religion* NewStatesman [Internet] Newstatesman Available at www.newstatesman.com [Accessed 09/01/18]

Macmurray J (1936) *The Structure of Religious Experience* Faber and Faber Limited pp.9-74

Ross T (2011) *'Belief in God is part of human nature' Oxford Study* [Internet] The Telegraph Available at www.telegraph.co.uk 8.17pm BST 12 May [Accessed 09/01/18].

Stavrakcopoulou F (Thanks Jong Jonathan University of Oxford) *'Are we wired to believe in a higher power?'* BBC iWonder [Internet] Available at www.bbc.co.uk [Accessed 09/01/18].

Religion as the 'Opium of the people'

Molyneux J (2008) *More than opium: Marxism and religion* International Socialism (Issue: 119)

Man makes region, religion does not make man

Marx, Karl and Engels, Frederick. (1846) *The German Ideology Part One* Student Edition Edited Arthur C.J (1974) Laurence & Wishart London p47

Marx, Karl (1859) *Preface To The Contribution of Political Economy* In Karl Marx and Fredrick Engels *Selected Works Volume 1*

Progress Publishers Moscow 1983 p503

Engels, Frederick (1883) *Engel's Burial Speech* [Internet] https://www.marxists.org [Accessed 5th August 2018]

Molyneux J (2008) *More than opium: Marxism and religion* International Socialism (Issue: 119)

Religion and alienation

Mandel, E and Novack, G (1974) *The Marxist Theory of Alienation* Second Edition Pathfinder Press New York p68

Marx, Karl (1852) *The Eighteenth Brumaire of Louis Bonaparte* In Karl Marx and Fredrick Engels *Selected Works Volume 1* Progress Publishers Moscow 1983

Valhalla Norse Mythology (2018) Available at: https://www.britannica.com [Accessed 6/8/18]

Fox, Mathew (2000) *One River many Wells* Jeremy P Tarcher/Putnam a member of Penguin Putnam Inc p1-11

John Macmurray: Marxism and the personal

Macmurray J (1933 October) *The Philosophy of Communism* Faber & Faber Limited

Wikipedia (2018) Miasma Theory Available at: < https://en.m.wikipedia.org > [Accessed 5/8/18].

Marx, Karl and Engels, Frederick. (1846) *The German Ideology Part One* Student Edition Edited Arthur C.J (1974) Laurence & Wishart London p123

Macmurray (1945) *Religion and Personal Relationship* May 10th *Search For A Faith* BBC Broadcasts

Macmurray J (1933 March) *Interpreting The Universe* Faber And Faber p124

Good religion, Bad religion

Macmurray J (1965) *Search for Reality in Religion* (Swarthmore Lecture) London: George Allen & Unwin Ltd.

Macmurray J (1935) *Creative Society* Student Christian Movement Press.

Personal Logic: The Self and Persons in Relation

Macmurray J (1991) *The Self As Agent* Humanity Books

Macmurray J (1999) *Persons in Relation* Humanity Books.

Macmurray J (1961) *Religion, Art & Science* Liverpool University Press

Marxism and Persons in Relation

Armstrong, K (2011) *Twelve Steps to a compassionate life* The Bodley Head

Macmurray J (1938) *The Clue To History* Student Christian Movement Press

Macmurray J (1932) *Freedom In The Modern World* (1992) Humanity Books.

Macmurray J (1999) *Persons in Relation* Humanity Books.

Fox, Mathew (2000) *One River many Wells* Jeremy P Tarcher/Putnam a member of Penguin Putnam Inc

Rohr, Richard (2015-2018) *Daily Meditations* Center for Action and Contemplation meditations@cac.org

A Kinder Politics and Why It Matters

Macmurray J (1933 March) *Interpreting The Universe* Faber And Faber

Macmurray, J (1945) *Search For A Faith* BBC Broadcasts

Macmurray, J (1945) *Search For A Faith 'Retrospect and Prospect* BBC Broadcast May 17th

Macmurray J (1991) *The Self As Agent* Humanity Books

Gandhi's Top 10 Fundamentals for Changing the World https://www.positivityblog.com 2:55 12/4/18

20 years after the TRC hearings South Africa's pain persists-Times LIVE https://www.timeslive.co.za, delivered by Google 14:10 7/5/18)

BIBLIOGRAPHY

Armstrong, K (1999) *A History of God* Vintage

Armstrong, K (2011) *Twelve Steps to a compassionate life* The Bodley Head

Balibar E (2007) *The Philosophy of Marx* Verso.

Bourgeault Cynthia(2008) *The Wisdom Jesus* Shambhala

Bourgeault, C (2016) *The Heart of Centering Prayer* Shambhala

Crossan John Dominic (1995) *Jesus: A Revolutionary Biography* HarperCollins

Conford P (1996) *The Personal World John Macmurray on self and society* Floris Books

Costello J E (2002)*John Macmurray A Biography* Edinburgh: Floris Books

Eagleton T (2009) *Reason, Faith and Revolution: Reflections on the God Debate* Yale.

Eisenstein, Charles (2013) *The More Beautiful World our Hearts Know is Possible* North Atlantic Books, Berkeley California

Engels, Frederick (1883) *Engel's Burial Speech* [Internet] https://

www.marxists.org [Accessed 5th August 2018]

Esher McIntosh(2004) *John Macmurray Selected Philosophical Writings* Imprint Academic

Fox, Mathew (2000) *One River many Wells* Jeremy P Tarcher/Putnam a member of Penguin Putnam Inc

Fraser G (2007) Terry Eagleton presents Jesus Christ *The Gospels* Texts selected and annotated by Giles Fraser Verso.

Macmurray J (1932) *Freedom In The Modern World* (1992) Humanity Books.

Macmurray J (1933 March) *Interpreting The Universe* Faber And Faber

Macmurray J (1933 October) *The Philosophy of Communism* Faber & Faber Limited

Macmurray J (1935) *Creative Society* Student Christian Movement Press.

Macmurray J (1935 June) *Reason and Emotion* Faber & Faber Limited

Macmurray J (1936) *The Structure of Religious Experience* Faber and Faber Limited

Macmurray J (1938) *The Clue To History* Student Christian Movement Press

Macmurray J (1939) *The Boundaries of Science* Faber & Faber Ltd

Macmurray J (1943) *Constructive Democracy* Faber & Faber Limited

Macmurray (1945) *Religion and Personal Relationship* May 10th *Search For A Faith* BBC Broadcasts

Macmurray J (1950) *Conditions of Freedom* Faber & Faber Ltd

Macmurray J (1961) *Religion, Art & Science* Liverpool University Press

Macmurray J (1965) *Search for Reality in Religion* (Swarthmore Lecture) London: George Allen & Unwin Ltd.

Macmurray J (1977) *The Philosophy of Jesus* (©John Macmurray, Friends Home Service Cmmittee, Friends House, Euston Road, London, NW1 2BJ)

Macmurray J (1991) *The Self As Agent* Humanity Books

Macmurray J (1932) *Freedom In The Modern World* (1992) Humanity Books.

Macmurray J (1999) *Persons in Relation* Humanity Books.

Mandel, E (1973) *An Introduction to Marxist Economic Theory* (Second Edition) New York: Pathfinder Press.

Mandel, E and Novack, G (1974) *The Marxist Theory of Alienation*

Jonathan Smith

Second Edition Pathfinder Press New York

Mandel, Ernest (1982) *Introduction to Marxism*(Second Edition) Pluto Press Ltd.

Marx, Karl and Engels, Frederick. (1846) *The German Ideology Part One* Student Edition Edited Arthur C.J (1974) Laurence & Wishart London

Marx, Karl (1852) *The Eighteenth Brumaire of Louis Bonaparte* In Karl Marx and Fredrick Engels *Selected Works Volume 1* Progress Publishers Moscow 1983

Marx, Karl (1859) *Preface To The Contribution of Political Economy* In Karl Marx and Fredrick Engels *Selected Works Volume 1* Progress Publishers Moscow 1983

Milavec, Aaron (2003) *The Didache Text ,Translation ,Analysis, and Commentary* Liturgical Press

Monbiot, George (2018) *Out of the Wreckage* Verso

Rock, H (2014) *God Needs Salvation A New Vision of God for the Twenty First Century* Christian Alternative.

Rohr, R and Feister, J (1996) *Jesus' Plan for a New World* St. Anthony Messenger Press

Rohr, R with Morrell, M (2016) *The Divine Dance* Society for Promoting Christian Knowledge

Wikipedia (2018) Miasma Theory Available at: < https://en.m.wikipedia.org > [Accessed 5/8/18].

Wilber, Ken (1996) *Up From Eden: A Transpersonal View of Human Evolution* Quest Books.

Wilber, Ken (1996) *A Brief History of Everything* Gateway.

Wilber, Ken (1995/2000) *Sex, Ecology, Spirituality The Spirit of Evolution* Shambhala

Paul Valley (2013) *Pope Francis Untying The Knots* Bloosmbury Publishing Plc.

Valhalla Norse Mythology (2018) Available at: https://www.britannica.com [Accessed 6/8/18]

NOTES

Jonathan Smith

NOTES

NOTES

Printed in Great Britain
by Amazon